Math Drills

Grade 2

Written by **Shannon Keeley**

Illustrations by **Viviana Garofoli**

FlashKids

An imprint of Sterling Children's Books

This book belongs to

_____

FLASH KIDS, STERLING, and the distinctive Sterling logo are registered trademarks of
Sterling Publishing Co., Inc.

Published by Sterling Publishing Co., Inc.
387 Park Avenue South, New York, NY 10016
Text and illustrations © 2006 by Flash Kids
Distributed in Canada by Sterling Publishing
c/o Canadian Manda Group, 165 Dufferin Street
Toronto, Ontario, Canada M6K 3H6
Distributed in the United Kingdom by GMC Distribution Services
Castle Place, 166 High Street, Lewes, East Sussex, England BN7 1XU
Distributed in Australia by Capricorn Link (Australia) Pty. Ltd.
P.O. Box 704, Windsor, NSW 2756, Australia

Sterling ISBN 978-1-4114-3451-6

Manufactured in China

Lot #:
14
07/16

For information about custom editions, special sales, premium and
corporate purchases, please contact Sterling Special Sales
Department at 800-805-5489 or specialsales@sterlingpublishing.com.

Cover design and production by Mada Design, Inc.

Dear Parent,

Learning to add and subtract is an important step in your child's educational development. This book will help your child learn the basics of addition, subtraction, and other important math skills covered in the second grade. Follow these simple steps to make the most of this workbook:

- Find a comfortable place where you and your child can work quietly together.
- Encourage your child to go at his or her own pace.
- Help your child with the problems if he or she needs it.
- Offer lots of praise and support.
- Let your child reward his or her work with the included stickers.
- Most of all, remember that learning should be fun! Enjoy this special time spent together.

Under the Big Top

Add. If the sum is even, color the area red.

If the sum is odd, color the area yellow.

1. 8
+7

2. 9
+5

3. 9
+4

4. 8
+8

5. 4
+7

6. 5
+5

7. 8
+9

8. 3
+9

Circus Switch!

You can switch the numbers in addition equations
and still get the same answer!

$$3 + 4 = 7$$
$$4 + 3 = 7$$

Switch the numbers and write the new equation.

1. $7 + 4 = \underline{}$
   $\underline{} + \underline{} = 11$

2. $9 + 7 = \underline{}$
   $\underline{} + \underline{} = 16$

3. $5 + 8 = \underline{}$
   $\underline{} + \underline{} = 13$

4. $8 + 6 = \underline{}$
   $\underline{} + \underline{} = 14$

5. $6 + 5 = \underline{}$
   $\underline{} + \underline{} = 11$

6. $3 + 2 = \underline{}$
   $\underline{} + \underline{} = 5$

Big Top Boss

Find the difference.
Use the letter next to each answer to solve the code.

Seahas
7/21/20

1. 12
  − 9
  ——
  3 **M**

2. 11
  − 7
  ——
  4 **G**

3. 18
  − 9
  ——
  9 **S**

4. 13
  − 8
  ——
  5 **R**

5. 16
  − 8
  ——
  8 **T**

6. 10
  − 9
  ——
  1 **A**

7. 15
  − 9
  ——
  6 **N**

8. 13
  − 6
  ——
  7 **R**

9. 10
  − 8
  ——
  2 **E**

10. 17
  − 7
  ——
  10 **I**

R I N G M A S T E R
5 10 6 4 3 1 9 8 2 7

Peanut Trail

Write the missing number for each equation.

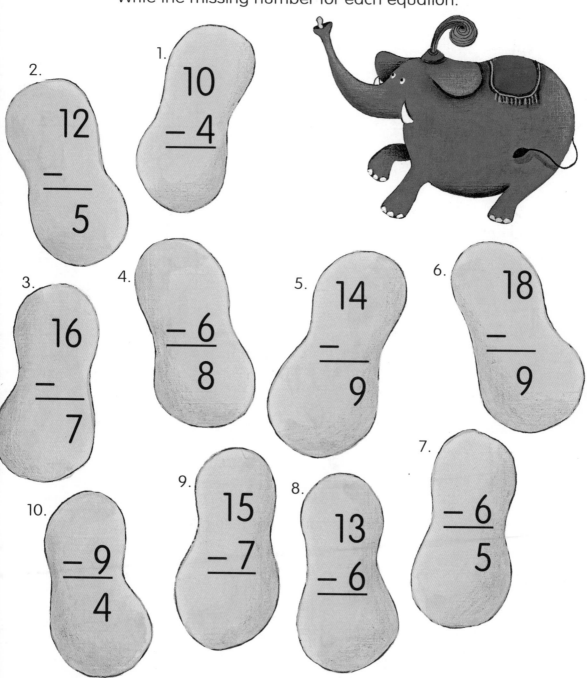

1.
$$\begin{array}{r} 10 \\ -\ 4 \\ \hline \end{array}$$

2.
$$\begin{array}{r} 12 \\ -\ \\ \hline 5 \end{array}$$

3.
$$\begin{array}{r} 16 \\ -\ \\ \hline 7 \end{array}$$

4.
$$\begin{array}{r} \\ -\ 6 \\ \hline 8 \end{array}$$

5.
$$\begin{array}{r} 14 \\ -\ \\ \hline 9 \end{array}$$

6.
$$\begin{array}{r} 18 \\ -\ \\ \hline 9 \end{array}$$

7.
$$\begin{array}{r} \\ -\ 6 \\ \hline 5 \end{array}$$

8.
$$\begin{array}{r} 13 \\ -\ 6 \\ \hline \end{array}$$

9.
$$\begin{array}{r} 15 \\ -\ 7 \\ \hline \end{array}$$

10.
$$\begin{array}{r} \\ -\ 9 \\ \hline 4 \end{array}$$

Daring Doubles

Learning doubles makes adding faster and easier.

$$\begin{array}{r} 1 \\ +1 \\ \hline 2 \end{array} \qquad \begin{array}{r} 2 \\ +2 \\ \hline 4 \end{array} \qquad \begin{array}{r} 3 \\ +3 \\ \hline 6 \end{array} \qquad \begin{array}{r} 4 \\ +4 \\ \hline 8 \end{array} \qquad \begin{array}{r} 5 \\ +5 \\ \hline 10 \end{array}$$

$$\begin{array}{r} 6 \\ +6 \\ \hline 12 \end{array} \qquad \begin{array}{r} 7 \\ +7 \\ \hline 14 \end{array} \qquad \begin{array}{r} 8 \\ +8 \\ \hline 16 \end{array} \qquad \begin{array}{r} 9 \\ +9 \\ \hline 18 \end{array}$$

Now find the sums for these doubles.

1. $\begin{array}{r} 4 \\ +4 \\ \hline \end{array}$ 2. $\begin{array}{r} 7 \\ +7 \\ \hline \end{array}$ 3. $\begin{array}{r} 8 \\ +8 \\ \hline \end{array}$ 4. $\begin{array}{r} 6 \\ +6 \\ \hline \end{array}$ 5. $\begin{array}{r} 2 \\ +2 \\ \hline \end{array}$ 6. $\begin{array}{r} 9 \\ +9 \\ \hline \end{array}$

Doubles Plus One

If you know your doubles, it's easy to add one more.

$$4 + 4 = 8$$
$$4 + 5 = 9$$
$$(4 + 1)$$

All the problems in the cage are doubles plus one.

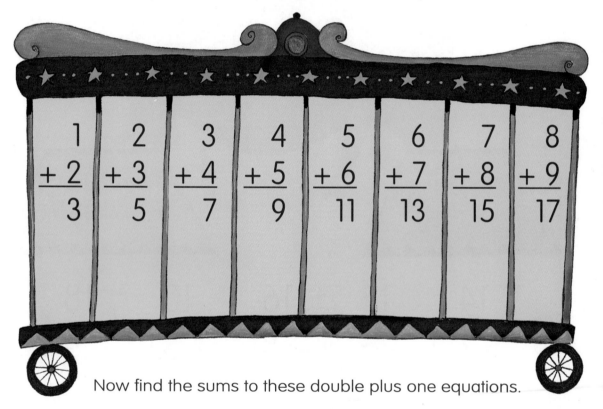

$$\begin{array}{r} 1 \\ +\,2 \\ \hline 3 \end{array}$$
$$\begin{array}{r} 2 \\ +\,3 \\ \hline 5 \end{array}$$
$$\begin{array}{r} 3 \\ +\,4 \\ \hline 7 \end{array}$$
$$\begin{array}{r} 4 \\ +\,5 \\ \hline 9 \end{array}$$
$$\begin{array}{r} 5 \\ +\,6 \\ \hline 11 \end{array}$$
$$\begin{array}{r} 6 \\ +\,7 \\ \hline 13 \end{array}$$
$$\begin{array}{r} 7 \\ +\,8 \\ \hline 15 \end{array}$$
$$\begin{array}{r} 8 \\ +\,9 \\ \hline 17 \end{array}$$

Now find the sums to these double plus one equations.

1. $\begin{array}{r} 4 \\ +\,5 \\ \hline \end{array}$
2. $\begin{array}{r} 2 \\ +\,3 \\ \hline \end{array}$
3. $\begin{array}{r} 7 \\ +\,8 \\ \hline \end{array}$
4. $\begin{array}{r} 5 \\ +\,6 \\ \hline \end{array}$
5. $\begin{array}{r} 1 \\ +\,2 \\ \hline \end{array}$
6. $\begin{array}{r} 8 \\ +\,9 \\ \hline \end{array}$

Subtraction Tricks

Subtraction is the opposite of addition.

You can turn around addition problems to get the answer.

Remember your addition facts with doubles and doubles plus one.

$6 + 6 = 12$

So, $12 - 6 = 6$

$6 + 7 = 13$

So, $13 - 6 = 7$

1. 14
    -7

2. 12
    -6

3. 16
    -8

4. 10
    -5

5. 18
    -9

6. 13
    -6

7. 9
    -4

8. 15
    -7

9. 11
    -5

10. 17
    -8

Fact Families

Addition and subtraction are part of the same family.

Knowing your addition facts can help you with subtraction problems.

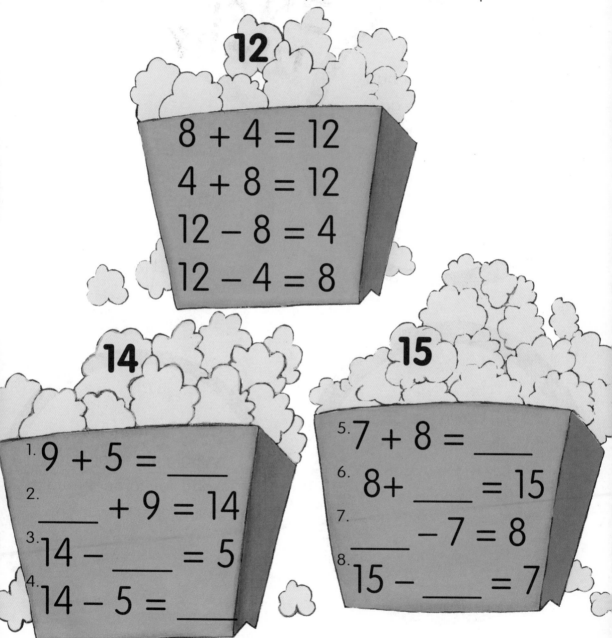

12

$$8 + 4 = 12$$
$$4 + 8 = 12$$
$$12 - 8 = 4$$
$$12 - 4 = 8$$

14

1. $9 + 5 =$ _____

2. _____ $+ 9 = 14$

3. $14 -$ _____ $= 5$

4. $14 - 5 =$ _____

15

5. $7 + 8 =$ _____

6. $8 +$ _____ $= 15$

7. _____ $- 7 = 8$

8. $15 -$ _____ $= 7$

Circus Stories

Read the sentences and figure out the answers. Show your work.

Ishan
12/19/19

1. The ringmaster had 14 peanuts. He gave 6 to the elephant. How many does he have left?

8

14 - 6 = 8

2. The juggler started with 6 balls. Then he juggled with 6 more! How many balls did he juggle altogether?

12

3. The clown had 15 balloons. He gave 8 away. How many does he have left?

7

4. The first lion tamer brought out 4 lions. The second lion tamer brought out 8 lions. How many lions are there in total?

12

Cage Count!

Fill in the missing numbers.

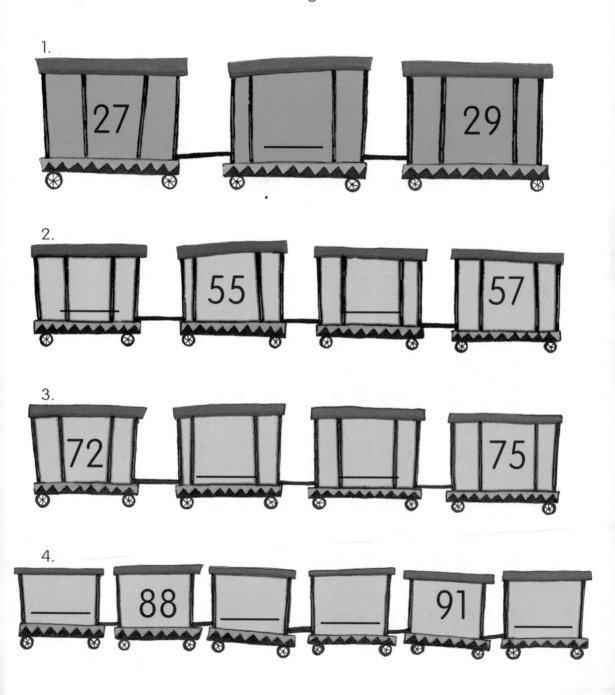

1. 27   ____   29

2. ____   55   ____   57

3. 72   ____   ____   75

4. ____   88   ____   ____   91   ____

Tent of Tens and Ones

Write how many groups of ten and ones there are.

Add the numbers.

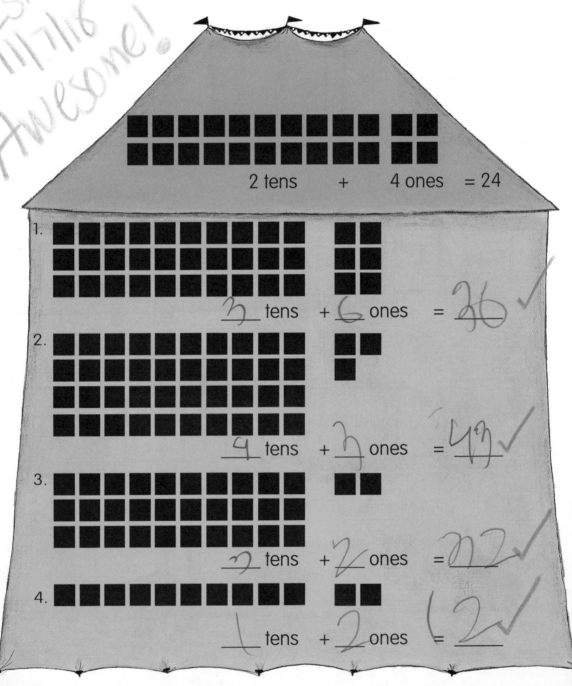

Ishan
11/7/16
Awesome!

2 tens + 4 ones = 24

1. __3__ tens + __6__ ones = __36__ ✓

2. __4__ tens + __7__ ones = __47__ ✓

3. __2__ tens + __2__ ones = __22__ ✓

4. __1__ tens + __2__ ones = __12__ ✓

Ishan 2/14/19

Juggler Joke

Add. Use the letter next to each answer to help solve the code.

9.
$$20 \\ +\ 9 \over 29$$
L

1.
$$17 \\ +\ 2 \over 19$$
V

2.
$$4\ ? \\ +\ 6 \over 49$$
L

8.
$$12 \\ +\ 4 \over 16$$
A

3.
$$45 \\ +\ 0 \over 45$$
H

7.
$$43 \\ +\ 4 \over 47$$
G

4.
$$56 \\ +\ 3 \over 59$$
I

6.
$$21 \\ +\ 7 \over 28$$
N

5.
$$30 \\ +\ 9 \over 39$$
B

H A V I N G
45 16 19 59 28 47

A B A L L
    39 16 29 49

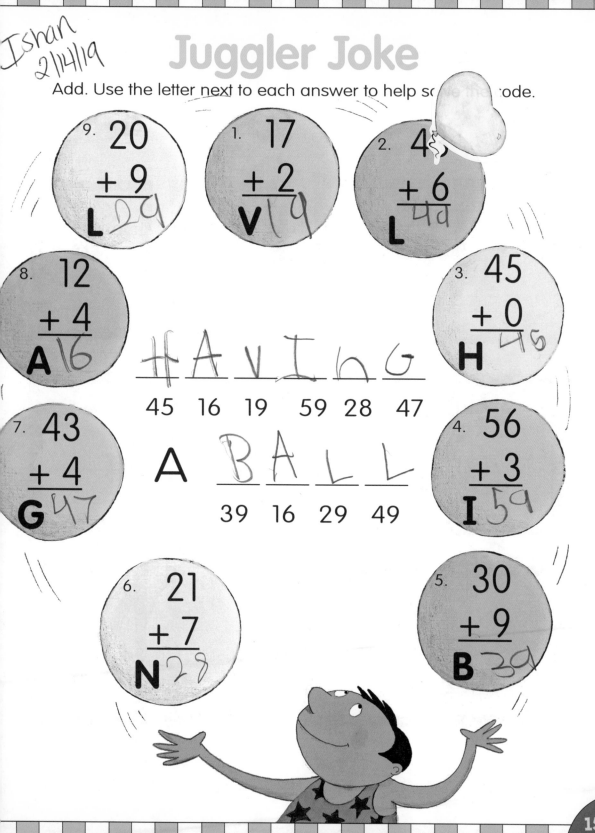

Monkey Math

Add the numbers and help the monkey get to the banana!

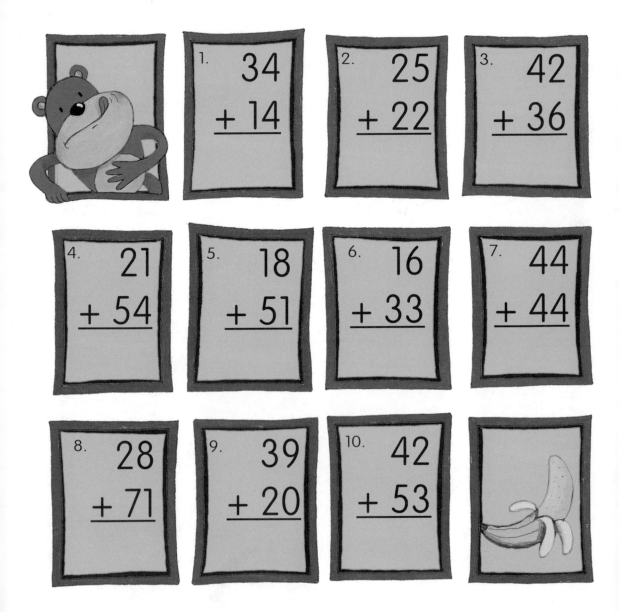

1. 34
   + 14

2. 25
   + 22

3. 42
   + 36

4. 21
   + 54

5. 18
   + 51

6. 16
   + 33

7. 44
   + 44

8. 28
   + 71

9. 39
   + 20

10. 42
    + 53

Number Line

You can use the number line to find the difference in a subtraction problem. Here, you are subtracting 6 from 14.
Start at 14. Jump back 6 spaces on the number line.
You will land on 8. This is the answer to the problem.

$$14 - 6 = 8$$

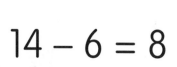

1 2 3 4 5 6 7 8 9 10 11 12 13 14 15 16 17 18 19 20

Use the number line to find the differences.

1 2 3 4 5 6 7 8 9 10 11 12 13 14 15 16 17 18 19 20

1. $20 - 3 =$

2. $16 - 6 =$

3. $17 - 4 =$

4. $14 - 10 =$

5. $7 - 4 =$

6. $12 - 8 =$

7. $20 - 7 =$

8. $19 - 5 =$

9. $18 - 2 =$

10. $15 - 6 =$

Math Path

Help the clown find his shoes.

Find the correct statements to make a path through the maze.

11 < 10

38 < 83

51 > 15

99 < 66

67 = 67

29 > 92

43 > 40

68 < 86

33 = 88

97 > 77

Top Hat Time

Write the time beneath each hat.

1. 2:00

2. 7:4 ?

3. 2:30

Draw the hands on the clocks to show the time.

4. 5:30

5. 8:30

6. 4:45

Time to Practice!

Draw hands to show the time each circus _____
started and stopped practicing.

START

STOP

The clown started
practicing _____
He practiced for 45 minutes.

2. The lion tamer started
practicing at 6:15.
He stopped 3 hours later.

START   **STOP**

3. The dancers started
practicing at 2:30.
They practiced for 30 minutes.

START   **STOP**

4. The monkeys started
practicing at 8:00.
They stopped $4\frac{1}{2}$
hours later.

START   **STOP**

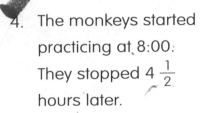

hours are short hand, Mins are long hand!
(Hint)

20

Regrouping Rings

Add the numbers by regrouping.

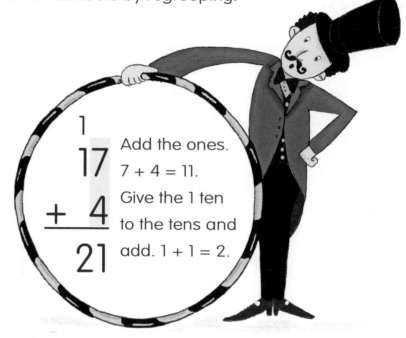

$$
\begin{array}{r}
1 \\
17 \\
+\ 4 \\
\hline
21
\end{array}
$$

Add the ones.
7 + 4 = 11.
Give the 1 ten
to the tens and
add. 1 + 1 = 2.

1.
$$
\begin{array}{r}
22 \\
+\ 8 \\
\hline
\end{array}
$$

2.
$$
\begin{array}{r}
18 \\
+\ 5 \\
\hline
\end{array}
$$

3.
$$
\begin{array}{r}
16 \\
+\ 6 \\
\hline
\end{array}
$$

4.
$$
\begin{array}{r}
37 \\
+\ 4 \\
\hline
\end{array}
$$

5.
$$
\begin{array}{r}
29 \\
+\ 5 \\
\hline
\end{array}
$$

6.
$$
\begin{array}{r}
36 \\
+\ 8 \\
\hline
\end{array}
$$

7.
$$
\begin{array}{r}
29 \\
+\ 4 \\
\hline
\end{array}
$$

8.
$$
\begin{array}{r}
19 \\
+\ 3 \\
\hline
\end{array}
$$

9.
$$
\begin{array}{r}
35 \\
+\ 7 \\
\hline
\end{array}
$$

10.
$$
\begin{array}{r}
48 \\
+\ 3 \\
\hline
\end{array}
$$

Balloon Fun

Add. If you had to regroup, color the balloon yellow.

If not, color the balloon green.

Saanas
7/21/20

1.
$$17$$
$$+ \ 9$$
$$26$$

2.
$$44$$
$$+ \ 5$$
$$49$$

3.
$$57$$
$$+ \ 4$$
$$61$$

4.
$$14$$
$$+ \ 8$$
$$22$$

5.
$$26$$
$$+ \ 5$$
$$31$$

6.
$$39$$
$$+ \ 6$$
$$45$$

7.
$$11$$
$$+ \ 8$$
$$19$$

8.
$$63$$
$$+ \ 6$$
$$60$$

9.
$$54$$
$$+ \ 3$$
$$57$$

10.
$$46$$
$$+ \ 7$$
$$53$$

$$\begin{array}{r} 17 \\ + 9 \\ \hline 16 \end{array}$$

Tightrope Race

Add and regroup. Mark off the answers on the tightropes as you go.
Find out who finishes first!

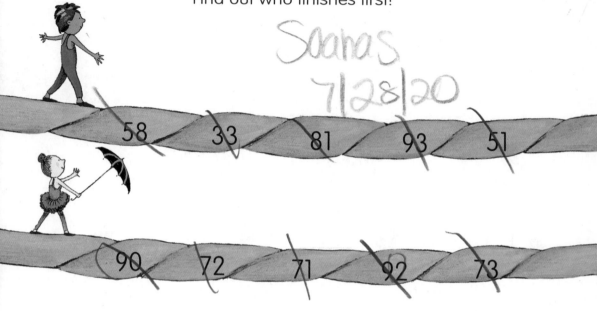

Saahas
7/28/20

58   33   81   93   51

90   72   71   92   73

1.
  24
+ 34
  58

2.
  16
+ 17
  33

3.
  34
+ 56
  90

4.
  65
+ 16
  81

5.
  47
+ 25
  72

6.
  38
+ 33
  71

7.
  77
+ 15
  92

8.
  65
+ 28
  93

9.
  48
+ 25
  73

10.
  24
+ 27
  51

Ice Cream Addition

Use regrouping to add. Write each answer inside the cone.

Saahas
7/23/20

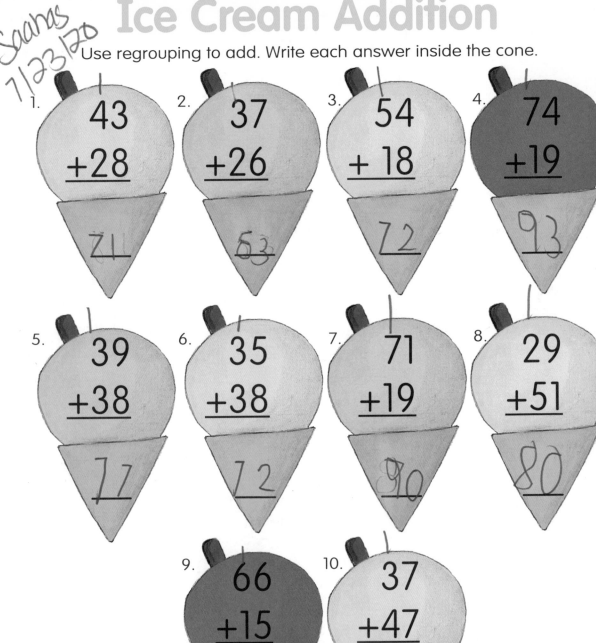

1.
43
+28
71

2.
37
+26
53

3.
54
+ 18
72

4.
74
+19
93

5.
39
+38
77

6.
35
+38
72

7.
71
+19
90

8.
29
+51
80

9.
66
+15
81

10.
37
+47
84

Plenty of Popcorn

Add. Find each sum inside the popcorn.

1.
$$29$$
$$+ 16$$

2.
$$67$$
$$+ 25$$

3.
$$72$$
$$+ 19$$

4.
$$64$$
$$+ 29$$

5.
$$18$$
$$+ 39$$

6.
$$47$$
$$+ 38$$

Ishan
12/6

Monkey Business

Read the sentences and solve the problems.
You may need to regroup. Show your work.

1. During the show, the monkeys clapped 28 times and jumped 32 times. How many times did they clap and jump altogether? __60__

2. The monkeys ate 14 bananas before the show and 27 bananas after the show. How many bananas did they eat altogether? __41__

3. At the beginning of the show, the monkeys were onstage for 35 minutes. At the end of the show, they were onstage for 17 minutes. How many minutes were they onstage altogether? __52__

9/20/18
Ishan

Circus Snacks

Count the coins to figure out the price for each.
Write the price on the tag.

1. 55 ✓

2. 30 ✓

3. 75 ✓

4. 50 ✓

Tent of Cents

A dollar is 100 cents. Count the coins and write how many cents there are. Compare the coin amount to the dollar and write <, >, or = .

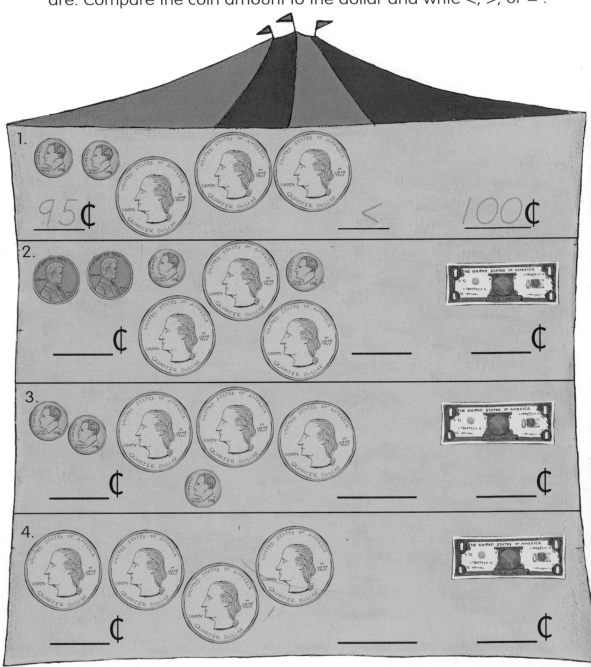

1. __95__ ¢ ___<___ __100__ ¢

2. _____ ¢ _____ _____ ¢

3. _____ ¢ _____ ¢

4. _____ ¢ _____ _____ ¢

Ride and Regroup

Use regrouping to solve each subtraction problem.

$$\begin{array}{r} {\scriptstyle 1\ 1} \\ 2\overset{1}{3} \\ -\ 6 \\ \hline 7 \end{array}\qquad\begin{array}{r} {\scriptstyle 1\ 1} \\ 2\overset{1}{3} \\ -\ 6 \\ \hline 1\ 7 \end{array}$$

To subtract the ones, you must take 1 from the tens. 13-6 = 7.

Now subtract the tens. 1-0 = 1.

1.
$$\begin{array}{r} 35 \\ -\ 7 \\ \hline 28 \end{array}$$

2.
$$\begin{array}{r} 15 \\ -\ 9 \\ \hline 6 \end{array}$$

3.
$$\begin{array}{r} 22 \\ -\ 8 \\ \hline 14 \end{array}$$

4.
$$\begin{array}{r} 41 \\ -\ 4 \\ \hline 37 \end{array}$$

5.
$$\begin{array}{r} 77 \\ -\ 9 \\ \hline 68 \end{array}$$

6.
$$\begin{array}{r} 52 \\ -\ 3 \\ \hline 49 \end{array}$$

7.
$$\begin{array}{r} 44 \\ -\ 6 \\ \hline 38 \end{array}$$

8.
$$\begin{array}{r} 21 \\ -\ 4 \\ \hline 17 \end{array}$$

9.
$$\begin{array}{r} 84 \\ -\ 9 \\ \hline 75 \end{array}$$

10.
$$\begin{array}{r} 74 \\ -\ 5 \\ \hline 69 \end{array}$$

6/24/20
Saahas

Regrouping Riddle

Use regrouping to solve the problems.

Use the letter next to each answer to help solve the riddle.

1.
```
  44
-  6
```
I 38

2.
```
  38
-  9
```
T 29

3.
```
  23
-  4
```
U 19

4.
```
  55
-  8
```
P 47

5.
```
  61
-  3
```
N 58

6.
```
  27
-  9
```
H 18

7.
```
  35
-  7
```
I 28

8.
```
  43
-  6
```
A 37

9.
```
  51
-  5
```
E 46

10.
```
  62
-  7
```
R 55

Why couldn't the acrobat make up his mind?

He was always <u>U P</u> <u>I N</u> <u>T H E</u> <u>A I R</u>.

19 47   38 58   29 18 46   37 28 55

Swinging Subtraction

Solve the problems.

1.
$$\begin{array}{r} 43 \\ -\ 29 \\ \hline \end{array}$$

2.
$$\begin{array}{r} 24 \\ -\ 15 \\ \hline \end{array}$$

3.
$$\begin{array}{r} 35 \\ -\ 28 \\ \hline \end{array}$$

4.
$$\begin{array}{r} 55 \\ -\ 26 \\ \hline \end{array}$$

5.
$$\begin{array}{r} 61 \\ -\ 42 \\ \hline \end{array}$$

6.
$$\begin{array}{r} 42 \\ -\ 33 \\ \hline \end{array}$$

7.
$$\begin{array}{r} 31 \\ -\ 19 \\ \hline \end{array}$$

8.
$$\begin{array}{r} 76 \\ -\ 48 \\ \hline \end{array}$$

9.
$$\begin{array}{r} 88 \\ -\ 19 \\ \hline \end{array}$$

10.
$$\begin{array}{r} 91 \\ -\ 66 \\ \hline \end{array}$$

Crazy for Cotton Candy

Solve each problem.

1. 64
    − 18

2. 27
    − 18

3. 33
    − 25

4. 36
    − 17

5. 56
    − 39

6. 81
    − 43

7. 92
    − 65

8. 79
    − 51

9. 45
    − 29

10. 22
    − 14

Subtraction Scoops

Subtract the numbers in the ice cream scoops.

Write each answer inside the cone.

1.
$$66 - 47$$

2.
$$21 - 13$$

3.
$$15 - 9$$

4.
$$84 - 37$$

5.
$$55 - 29$$

6.
$$94 - 48$$

7.
$$71 - 42$$

8.
$$63 - 27$$

9.
$$35 - 16$$

10.
$$78 - 29$$

Clown Capers

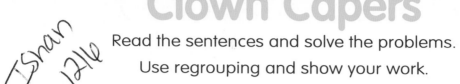

Read the sentences and solve the problems.
Use regrouping and show your work.

Ishan
12/6

1. There were 24 clowns in the car. The car stopped and 16 got out. How many clowns are still in the car? __18 X 12__

3
42
-26
16

2. The clown had 42 balloons. A big gust of wind came, and he let 26 of the balloons fly away. How many balloons does he have left? ___16___   42-26 =

3. Carl the Clown has a tie with 55 polka dots on it. Chris the Clown has a tie with 70 polka dots. How many more polka dots are on Chris the Clown's tie? __25 X 35 X 15__

4. In the first show, 33 kids took pictures of Carl the Clown. In the second, 60 kids took pictures of him. How many more kids took pictures in the second show? __37 X 33 X 27__

Cotton Candy Count

Cotton candy costs 32 cents at the circus.

Subtract to figure out how much change each child should get.

Then circle the coins that make the exact change.

1. Dave paid 40¢   How much change?

$$
\begin{array}{r}
3\,40 \\
-\ 32 \\
\hline
08¢
\end{array}
$$

2. Anna paid 50¢   How much change?

$$
\begin{array}{r}
4\,50 \\
-\ 32 \\
\hline
18
\end{array}
$$

3. Grace paid 35¢   How much change?

$$
\begin{array}{r}
35 \\
-\ 32 \\
\hline
03
\end{array}
$$

4. Parker paid 45¢   How much change?

$$
\begin{array}{r}
45 \\
-\ 32 \\
\hline
13
\end{array}
$$

35

Clown's Missing Coins

Figure out which coin is missing in each group.

Draw a line to help the clown find the missing coin.

1. 51¢

2. 52¢

3. 36¢

4. 43¢

Shoelace Lengths

Cut out the ruler.

Measure each shoelace and write the length in centimeters.

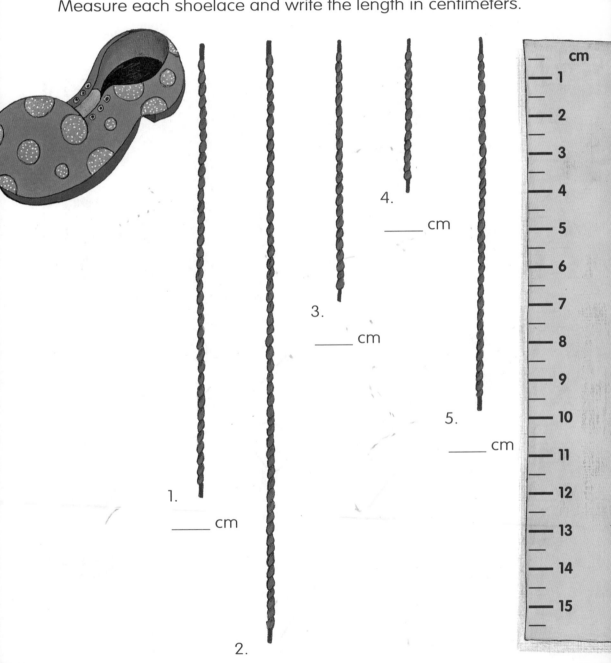

4.

_____ cm

3.

_____ cm

5.

_____ cm

1.

_____ cm

2.

_____ cm

	cm
	1
	2
	3
	4
	5
	6
	7
	8
	9
	10
	11
	12
	13
	14
	15

Perimeter Problems

The distance around an object is the **perimeter**. Measure each side of the object with the ruler and write the length in centimeters. Then add all the sides together to get the perimeter.

cm
1
2
3
4
5
6
7
8
9
10
11
12
13
14
15

1. _____ cm

cm   cm

_____ cm

perimeter = _____ cm

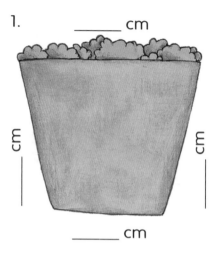

2. _____ cm

cm   cm

_____ cm

perimeter = _____ cm

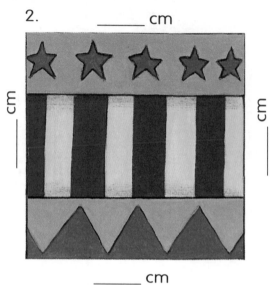

3. cm _____ cm

cm
cm

cm _____ cm

perimeter = _____ cm

4.

cm   cm

_____ cm

perimeter = _____ cm

Jumping Dogs

Cut out the ruler. Measure the distance that each dog can jump.
Write the distance in inches.

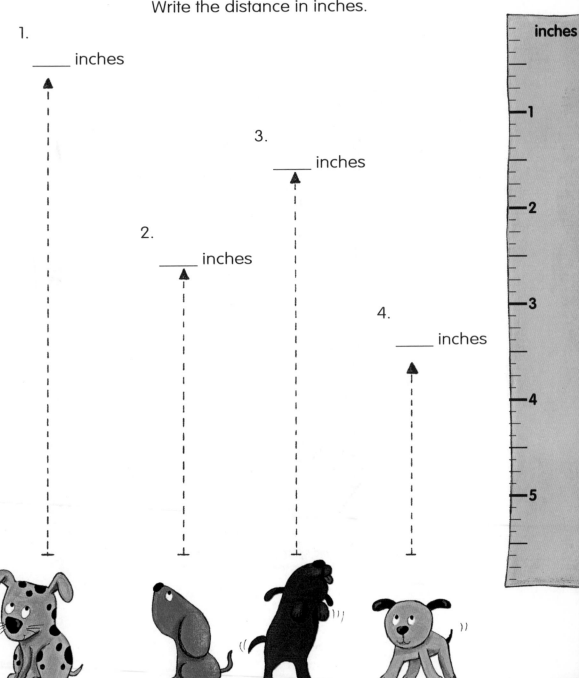

1.

_____ inches

2.

_____ inches

3.

_____ inches

4.

_____ inches

inches

1

2

3

4

5

Let's Monkey Around

Use the ruler to measure the distance around the monkey cage. Write how many inches each side is. Then add the sides together and write the perimeter.

_____ inches

inches

inches

_____ inches

perimeter = _____

inches

1

2

3

4

5

Triple Digit Time!

Count and write how many hundreds, tens, and ones are in each group. Then write the number.

1.

<u>2</u> hundreds   <u>3</u> tens   <u>2</u> ones   <u>232</u>

2.

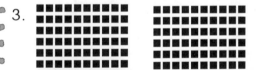 ___ hundreds   ___ tens   ___ ones   _____

3.

___ hundreds   ___ tens   ___ ones   _____

4.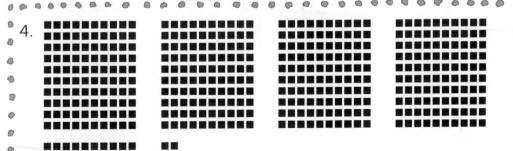

___ hundreds   ___ tens   ___ ones   _____

Tumbling Triples

Solve the problems.

1. 426
   + 21
   447

2. 254
   + 13
   267

3. 753
   + 36
   789

4. 506
   + 91
   597

5. 630
   + 49
   679

6. 444
   + 232
   676

7. 837
   + 104
   941

8. 340
   + 349
   689

9. 721
   + 112
   833

10. 213
    + 585
    798

42

Highwire Hundreds

Use regrouping to add the numbers.

$$1$$
$$326$$
$$+ 236$$
$$\overline{562}$$

Add the ones. 6 + 6 = 12

Regroup by giving 1 ten to the tens.

1 + 2 + 3 = 6

Add the hundreds. 3 + 2 = 5

8/24/20 Saahas

1. 435
  + 336
   771

2. 414
  + 207
   824

3. 546
  + 128
   674

4. 378
  + 514
   891

5. 656
  + 329
   985

6. 102
  + 629
   731

7. 757
  + 107
   864

8. 206
  + 227
   433

9. 746
  + 237
   983

10. 707
  + 238
   945

Tank of Triples

Add and regroup to solve the problems.

```
  1
 261
+373
 634
```

Add the ones. 1 + 3 = 4
Add the tens. 6 + 7 = 13.
Regroup the tens.
Add the hundreds. 1 + 2 + 3 = 6

1.
```
 461
+372
 813
```

2.
```
 550
+289
 839
```

3.
```
 291
+444
 735
```

4.
```
 673
+252
 925
```

5.
```
 782
+130
 912
```

6.
```
 150
+477
 627
```

7.
```
 670
+241
 911
```

8.
```
 268
+261
 529
```

9.
```
 351
+272
 623
```

Clown Code 8171

Solve the problems.

Use the letter next to each answer to help solve the riddle.

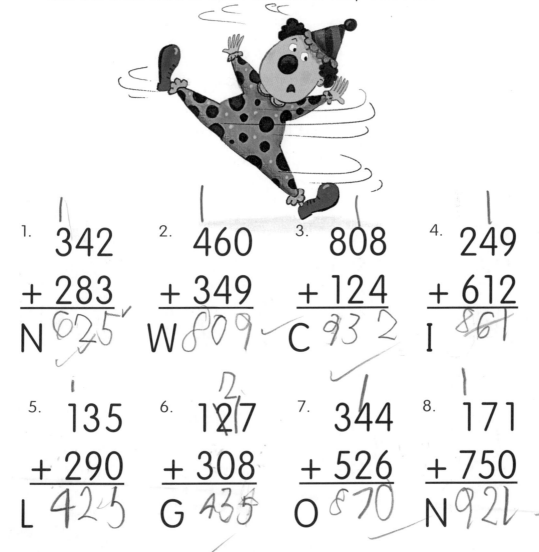

1.
$$342 + 283$$
N 625

2.
$$460 + 349$$
W 809

3.
$$808 + 124$$
C 932

4.
$$249 + 612$$
I 861

5.
$$135 + 290$$
L 425

6.
$$127 + 308$$
G 435

7.
$$344 + 526$$
O 870

8.
$$171 + 750$$
N 921

Why was the clown dizzy?
He couldn't stop C L O W N I N G around!

932 425 870 809 921 861 625 435

Hot Dog Hundreds

Use regrouping to add the numbers.

```
  1 1
  256
+ 176
  432
```

Sometimes you have to regroup
the ones and the tens.
Add the ones. 6 + 6 = 12.
Regroup the ones.
Add the tens. 1 + 5 + 7 = 13.
Regroup the tens.
Add the hundreds. 1 + 2 + 1 = 4

1.
```
  266
+ 145
```

2.
```
  345
+ 345
```

3.
```
  547
+ 274
```

4.
```
  506
+ 249
```

5.
```
  349
+ 452
```

6.
```
  192
+ 440
```

7.
```
  146
+ 187
```

8.
```
  377
+ 293
```

9.
```
  356
+ 299
```

10.
```
  188
+ 232
```

Circus Seats

Read the sentences and solve the problems. Show your work.

1. On Saturday, 230 of the circus seats were filled.
   On Sunday 455 of the seats were filled.
   How many seats were filled over the weekend? _____

2. The first row of the circus has 128 seats.
   The second row has 150 seats. How many
   seats are in the first and second rows altogether?

   _____

3. Section A inside the tent has 360 seats.
   Section B has the same number as Section A.
   How many seats are in sections A and B altogether?

   _____

4. Inside the circus tent there are 368
   blue seats and 266 red seats. How many
   blue and red seats are there in all? _____

Drum Roll

18/7/20

Subtract to find the answers.

1. 543
    − 33
    ——
    510

2. 289
    − 76
    ——
    213

3. 167
    − 42
    ——
    125

4. 747
    − 25
    ——
    222

5. 555
    − 31
    ——
    524

6. 745
    − 122
    ——
    623

7. 458
    − 243
    ——
    216

8. 975
    − 643
    ——
    332

9. 635
    − 324
    ——
    311

10. 538
    − 117
    ——
    521

Subtraction on Stilts

Use regrouping to subtract the numbers.

8/7/20
Saahas

$$\begin{array}{r} 5\ 11 \\ 26\!\!\!/1 \\ -\ 125 \\ \hline 136 \end{array}$$

Regroup to subtract the ones.

$11 - 5 = 6$.

Subtract the tens.

$5 - 2 = 3$.

Subtract the hundreds.

$2 - 1 = 1$.

1.
$$\begin{array}{r} 435 \\ -\ 219 \\ \hline 654 \end{array}$$

2.
$$\begin{array}{r} 294 \\ -\ 138 \\ \hline 334 \end{array}$$

3.
$$\begin{array}{r} 456 \\ -\ 339 \\ \hline 117 \end{array}$$

4.
$$\begin{array}{r} 562 \\ -\ 234 \\ \hline 328 \end{array}$$

5.
$$\begin{array}{r} 675 \\ -\ 438 \\ \hline 237 \end{array}$$

6.
$$\begin{array}{r} 345 \\ -\ 109 \\ \hline 236 \end{array}$$

7.
$$\begin{array}{r} 843 \\ -\ 625 \\ \hline 218 \end{array}$$

8.
$$\begin{array}{r} 965 \\ -\ 708 \\ \hline 257 \end{array}$$

9.
$$\begin{array}{r} 520 \\ -\ 112 \\ \hline 408 \end{array}$$

10.
$$\begin{array}{r} 965 \\ -\ 648 \\ \hline 317 \end{array}$$

Regroup Roar

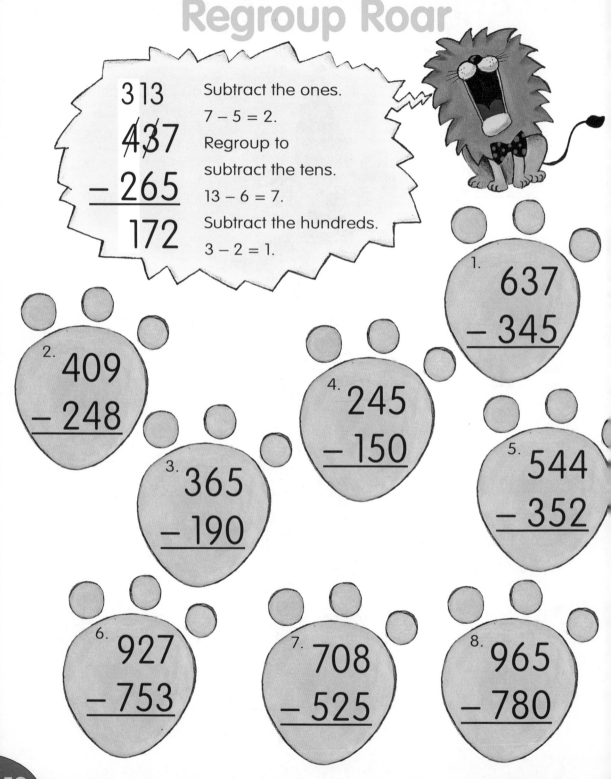

$\begin{array}{r} 3\,13 \\ 4\cancel{3}7 \\ -\ 265 \\ \hline 172 \end{array}$

Subtract the ones.
7 − 5 = 2.
Regroup to
subtract the tens.
13 − 6 = 7.
Subtract the hundreds.
3 − 2 = 1.

1.
$\begin{array}{r} 637 \\ -\ 345 \\ \hline \end{array}$

2.
$\begin{array}{r} 409 \\ -\ 248 \\ \hline \end{array}$

4.
$\begin{array}{r} 245 \\ -\ 150 \\ \hline \end{array}$

3.
$\begin{array}{r} 365 \\ -\ 190 \\ \hline \end{array}$

5.
$\begin{array}{r} 544 \\ -\ 352 \\ \hline \end{array}$

6.
$\begin{array}{r} 927 \\ -\ 753 \\ \hline \end{array}$

7.
$\begin{array}{r} 708 \\ -\ 525 \\ \hline \end{array}$

8.
$\begin{array}{r} 965 \\ -\ 780 \\ \hline \end{array}$

The Great Tamer

Subtract and regroup to solve each pair of problems.
Compare the answers and write the >, <, or = sign.

1.
$$344 - 206 = 138$$ $$>$$ $$382 - 276 = 106$$

2.
$$825 - 685$$ $$456 - 328$$

3.
$$650 - 321$$ $$547 - 253$$

4.
$$433 - 281$$ $$342 - 190$$

5.
$$749 - 578$$ $$883 - 608$$

Subtraction Spotlight

Regroup to solve each problem.

$$
\begin{array}{r}
5\ 12\ 12 \\
\cancel{632} \\
-\ 265 \\
\hline
367
\end{array}
$$

Regroup to subtract the ones.
$12 - 5 = 7.$
Regroup to subtract the tens.
$12 - 6 = 6.$
Subtract the hundreds.
$5 - 2 = 3.$

1.
$$
\begin{array}{r}
652 \\
-\ 365 \\
\hline
\end{array}
$$

2.
$$
\begin{array}{r}
436 \\
-\ 147 \\
\hline
\end{array}
$$

3.
$$
\begin{array}{r}
705 \\
-\ 246 \\
\hline
\end{array}
$$

4.
$$
\begin{array}{r}
843 \\
-\ 577 \\
\hline
\end{array}
$$

5.
$$
\begin{array}{r}
550 \\
-\ 365 \\
\hline
\end{array}
$$

6.
$$
\begin{array}{r}
312 \\
-\ 125 \\
\hline
\end{array}
$$

7.
$$
\begin{array}{r}
244 \\
-\ 156 \\
\hline
\end{array}
$$

8.
$$
\begin{array}{r}
503 \\
-\ 299 \\
\hline
\end{array}
$$

9.
$$
\begin{array}{r}
922 \\
-\ 338 \\
\hline
\end{array}
$$

10.
$$
\begin{array}{r}
480 \\
-\ 195 \\
\hline
\end{array}
$$

Circus Shop

Read the sentences and solve the problems. Show your work.

1. The circus shop had 450 flashlights before the show. They sold 268 flashlights during the show. How many flashlights did not get sold? _____182_____

2. During Friday night's show, 150 people bought balloons from the circus shop. There were 325 balloons for sale before the show. How many balloons were left after the show?

   _____175_____

3. The circus shop had 612 posters for sale. They sold 342 posters over the weekend. How many posters were left on Monday?

   _____270_____

4. On Saturday night, 623 people bought tickets to the circus show. There were 800 tickets available for that show. How many tickets were not sold? _____177_____

Traveling Time

Draw the hands and write the times the circus arrived in each town.

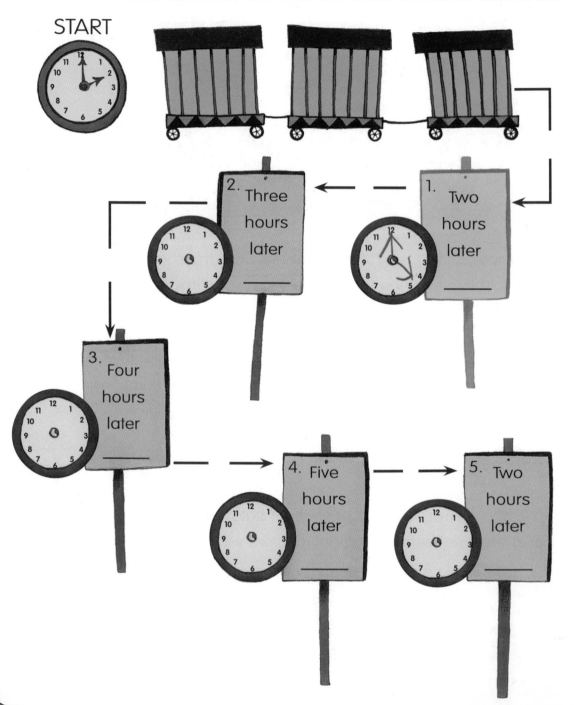

START

1. Two hours later
_____

2. Three hours later
_____

3. Four hours later
_____

4. Five hours later
_____

5. Two hours later
_____

Circus Schedule

Use the schedule to figure out how long each circus act performs. Then match each performer with the correct length of time.

clowns	6:00 – 6:45
acrobats	7:15 – 7:30
monkeys	7:45 – 8:15
elephants	8:30 – 9:30

1.

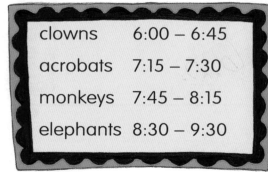

15 minutes

2.

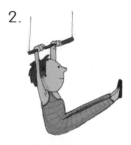

1 hour

3.

30 minutes

4.

45 minutes

Ishan
11/9/18

Clown Costumes

Count the money to figure out the price of each item.

Write the price on the tag.

1. $6.25

2. $5.70

3. $4.20

4. $3

5. $7.06

6. $1.76

More Clown Costumes

Use the prices on page 56 to solve the problems.

1. Harry the Clown bought  and .

   How much did he spend? _____

2. Casey the Clown had $8.50. She bought  and

   . How much did she have left? _____

3. Wes the Clown had $9.75. He bought and .

   How much did he have left? _____

Amazing Animal Acts

People voted for their favorite animal act from the circus.
Follow the directions to help complete the graph.

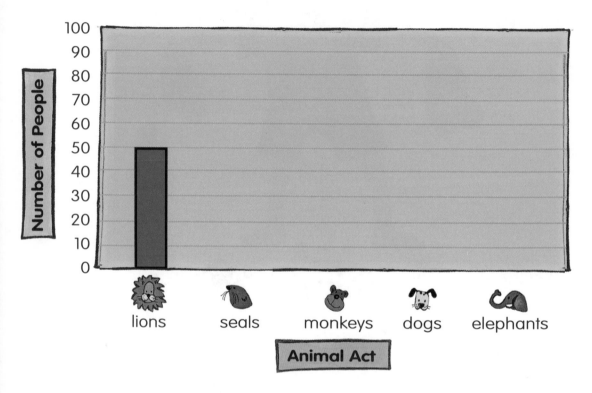

The first bar shows that 50 people voted for the lions.

1. Make a bar to show that 40 people voted for the seals.

2. Draw a bar showing that 70 people voted for the monkeys.

3. Make a bar to show that 20 people voted for the dogs.

4. Draw a bar showing that 90 people voted for the elephants.

More Amazing Animal Acts

Use the graph on page 58 to solve the word problems.

Show your work.

1. How many more people voted for the monkeys than the lions? _____

2. Which animal act received the most votes? _____

3. How many people voted for the lions, seals, and dogs altogether? _____

4. Which animal act got the least number of votes? _____

5. How many more people voted for the seals than the dogs? _____

6. If each person voted only once, how many people voted for the animals altogether? _____

Circus Shapes

Count how many of each shape you see in the picture.
Then draw a line to the word that describes each shape.

5/29/20
Saahas.

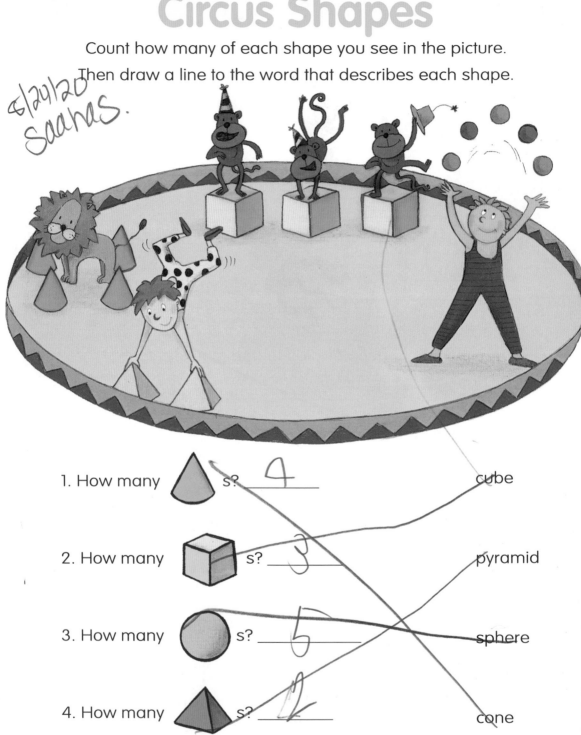

1. How many ⬤s? _____4_____   cube

2. How many ⬛s? _____3_____   pyramid

3. How many ⬤s? _____5_____   sphere

4. How many ▲s? _____2_____   cone

60

Runaway Circus!

Use the map to find the runaway circus animals.

Write the numbers and letters that show where each animal is.

1.   2.   3.

_____ _____   _____ _____   _____ _____

Find each animal and write its name.

4. 2A _____

5. 1C _____

6. 4E _____

Answer Key

Page 4

Page 5
1. 7 + 4 = <u>11</u> ;
     <u>4</u> + <u>7</u> = 11
2. 9 + 7 = <u>16</u> ;
     <u>7</u> + <u>9</u> = 16
3. 5 + 8 = <u>13</u> ;
     <u>8</u> + <u>5</u> = 13
4. 8 + 6 = <u>14</u> ;
     <u>6</u> + <u>8</u> = 14
5. 6 + 5 = <u>11</u> ;
     <u>5</u> + <u>6</u> = 11
6. 3 + 2 = <u>5</u> ;
     <u>2</u> + <u>3</u> = 5

Page 6
1. 3
2. 4
3. 9
4. 5
5. 8
6. 1
7. 6
8. 7
9. 2
10. 10
RINGMASTER

Page 7
1. 6
2. 7
3. 9
4. 14
5. 5
6. 9
7. 11
8. 7
9. 8
10. 13

Page 8
1. 8
2. 14
3. 16
4. 12
5. 4
6. 18

Page 9
1. 9
2. 5
3. 15
4. 11
5. 3
6. 17

Page 10
1. 7
2. 6
3. 8
4. 5
5. 9
6. 7
7. 5
8. 8
9. 6
10. 9

Page 11
1. 9 + 5 = 14
2. 5 + 9 = 14
3. 14 − 9 = 5
4. 14 − 5 = 9
5. 7 + 8 = 15
6. 8 + 7 = 15
7. 15 − 7 = 8
8. 15 − 8 = 7

Page 12
1. 14 − 6 = 8
2. 6 + 6 = 12
3. 15 − 8 = 7
4. 4 + 8 = 12

Page 13
1. 28
2. 54 56
3. 73 74
4. 87 89 90 92

Page 14
1. 3 tens + 6 ones = 36
2. 4 tens + 3 ones = 43
3. 3 tens + 2 ones = 32
4. 1 tens + 2 ones = 12

Page 15
1. 19
2. 49
3. 45
4. 59
5. 39
6. 28
7. 47
8. 16
9. 29
HAVING A BALL

Page 16
1. 48
2. 47
3. 78
4. 75
5. 69
6. 49
7. 88
8. 99
9. 59
10. 95

Page 17
1. 17
2. 10
3. 13
4. 4
5. 3
6. 4
7. 13
8. 14
9. 16
10. 9

Page 18
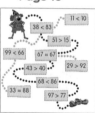

38 < 83
11 < 10
51 > 15
99 < 66
67 = 67
29 > 92
43 > 40
68 < 86
33 = 88
97 > 77

Page 19
1. 2:00
2. 12:45
3. 7:30
4.
5.
6.

Page 20
1. Start: Stop:
2. Start: Stop:
3. Start: Stop:

4. Start: Stop:

Page 21
1. 30
2. 23
3. 22
4. 41
5. 34
6. 44
7. 33
8. 22
9. 42
10. 51

Page 22
1. 26; yellow
2. 49; green
3. 61; yellow
4. 22; yellow
5. 31; yellow
6. 45; yellow
7. 19; green
8. 69; green
9. 57; green
10. 53; yellow

Page 23
1. 58
2. 33
3. 90
4. 81
5. 72
6. 71
7. 92
8. 93
9. 73
10. 51

Page 24
1. 71
2. 63
3. 72
4. 93
5. 77
6. 73
7. 90
8. 80
9. 81
10. 84

Page 25
1. 45
2. 92
3. 91
4. 93
5. 57
6. 85

Page 26
1. 28 + 32 = 60
2. 14 + 27 = 41
3. 35 + 17 = 52

Page 27
1. 55¢
2. 32¢
3. 75¢
4. 50¢

Page 28
2. 97 < 100
3. 105 > 100
4. 100 = 100

Page 29
1. 28
2. 6
3. 14
4. 37
5. 68
6. 49
7. 38
8. 17
9. 75
10. 69

Page 30
1. 38
2. 29
3. 19
4. 47
5. 58
6. 18
7. 28
8. 37
9. 46
10. 55
UP IN THE AIR

Page 31
1. 14
2. 9
3. 7
4. 29
5. 19
6. 9
7. 12
8. 28
9. 69
10. 25

Answer Key

Page 32
1. 46
2. 9
3. 8
4. 19
5. 17
6. 38
7. 27
8. 28
9. 16
10. 8

Page 33
1. 19
2. 8
3. 6
4. 47
5. 26
6. 46
7. 29
8. 36
9. 19
10. 49

Page 34
1. 24 − 16 = 8
2. 42 − 26 = 16
3. 70 − 55 = 15
4. 60 − 33 = 27

Page 35
1. 8 cents,

2. 18 cents,

3. 3 cents,

4. 13 cents,

Page 36
1.
2.
3.
4.

Page 37
1. 12 cm
2. 16 cm
3. 7 cm
4. 4 cm
5. 10 cm

Page 38
1. 16
2. 24
3. 12
4. 15

Page 39
1. 5 inches
2. 3 inches
3. 4 inches
4. 2 inches

Page 40
perimeter = 18 inches

Page 41
2. 3 hundreds 4 tens
   0 ones, 340
3. 1 hundred 6 tens
   5 ones, 165
4. 4 hundreds 3 tens
   2 ones, 432

Page 42
1. 447
2. 267
3. 789
4. 597
5. 679
6. 676
7. 941
8. 689
9. 833
10. 798

Page 43
1. 771
2. 621
3. 674
4. 892
5. 985
6. 731
7. 864
8. 433
9. 983
10. 945

Page 44
1. 833
2. 839
3. 735
4. 925
5. 912
6. 627
7. 911
8. 529
9. 623

Page 45
1. 625
2. 809
3. 932
4. 861
5. 425
6. 435
7. 870
8. 921
CLOWNING

Page 46
1. 411
2. 690
3. 821
4. 755
5. 801
6. 632
7. 333
8. 670
9. 655
10. 420

Page 47
1. 230 + 455 = 685
2. 128 + 150 = 278
3. 360 + 360 = 720
4. 368 + 266 = 634

Page 48
1. 510
2. 213
3. 125
4. 722
5. 524
6. 623
7. 215
8. 332
9. 311
10. 421

Page 49
1. 216
2. 156
3. 117
4. 328
5. 237
6. 236
7. 218
8. 257
9. 408
10. 317

Page 50
1. 292
2. 161
3. 175
4. 95
5. 192
6. 174
7. 183
8. 185

Page 51
2. 140 > 128
3. 329 > 294
4. 152 = 152
5. 171 < 275

Page 52
1. 287
2. 289
3. 459
4. 266
5. 185
6. 187
7. 88
8. 204
9. 584
10. 285

Page 53
1. 450 − 268 = 182
2. 325 − 150 = 175
3. 612 − 342 = 270
4. 800 − 623 = 177

Page 54
1.
2.
3.
4.
5.

Page 55
1. 45 minutes
2. 15 minutes
3. 30 minutes
4. 1 hour

Page 56
1. $6.25
2. $5.50
3. $4.20
4. $3.35
5. $7.06
6. $1.75

Page 57
1. $8.81
2. 95¢
3. $2.50

Page 58
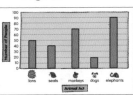

Page 59
1. 70 − 50 = 20
   people
2. elephants
3. 50 + 40 + 20 =
   110 people
4. dogs
5. 40 − 20 = 20
   people
6. 50 + 40 + 70 + 20
   + 90 = 270

Page 60
1. 4 cones
2. 3 cubes
3. 5 spheres
4. 2 pyramids

Page 61
1. 5B
2. 2B
3. 3D
4. monkey
5. lion
6. dog

Great job,

_____ !

(Name)

You did super work learning all the Grade 2 math skills!